The Story of the Car

Written by **GILES CHAPMAN**

Illustrated by **US NOW**

wren
&rook

1769

1886

1892

1900

1922

1934

1950

199

First published in Great Britain in 2017 by Wren & Rook

ISBN: 978 1 5263 6026 7
E-book ISBN: 978 1 5263 6078 6
10 9 8 7 6 5 4 3 2 1

Wren & Rook
An imprint of
Hachette Children's Group
Part of Hodder & Stoughton
Carmelite House
50 Victoria Embankment
London EC4Y 0DZ

An Hachette UK Company
www.hachette.co.uk
www.hachettechildrens.co.uk

Publishing Director: Debbie Foy
Editor: Liza Miller
Designers: Sidonie Beresford-Browne and Sarah Finan

Printed in China

Contents

PANHARD ET LEVASSOR

FORD MODEL T

MERCEDES-BENZ SSK

CADILLAC
ELDORADO

MINI COOPER

A Driving Ambition

EVER SINCE ITS INVENTION, THE CAR HAS HELPED TO RESHAPE AND DEFINE THE WORLD WE LIVE IN.

The world's roads began as routes for pedestrians and simple wooden vehicles pulled by animals. Indeed, the word 'car' originated from the term 'horseless carriage'. But since the introduction of the automobile, roads have been completely reinvented. Today's motorists can enjoy a smooth and speedy ride on motorways and highways, or seek out roads with stunning scenery, thrilling turns and undulating terrain.

Over the last 140 years, there have been many different styles and models of car, but they all share two grand ambitions: effortless speed and unlimited freedom for the driver.

CORD 810

LOTUS ESPRIT

PORSCHE 959

SMART CITY-COUPÉ

BMW i8

The First Automobile

IT'S HARD TO IMAGINE A WORLD BEFORE THE CAR, BUT THE AUTOMOBILE
AS WE KNOW IT HAS NOT BEEN AROUND FOR LONG.

In 1769, a Frenchman called Nicolas-Joseph Cugnot built the very first
steam-powered road vehicle. It was a strange contraption, and passers-by
were alarmed by its loud hissing and explosions of steam.

Cugnot's metal beast rolled along at 3 kilometres per hour – slower than the
average walking speed – and was difficult and dangerous to control. Steam-
powered vehicles were a far cry from the sleek, speedy machines of today.

THE INTERNAL COMBUSTION ENGINE

However, a century later, in Germany, a much more promising discovery was made. In 1876, the German inventor Nikolaus Otto designed the internal combustion engine. His idea was to mix oxygen and fuel inside a chamber, then use a spark to cause a mini explosion. This explosion made a piston bounce up and down, which in turn forced a shaft to turn a wheel.

1886

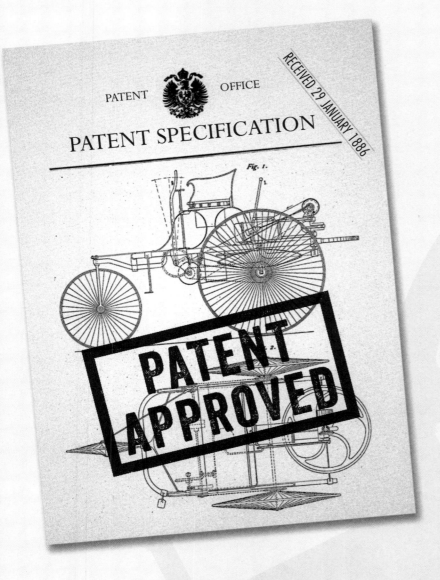

THE FIRST CAR

Otto's invention was called a four-stroke engine, and by 1886, two other German designers had created high-speed versions. Their names were Karl Benz and Gottlieb Daimler. Benz and Daimler developed their inventions at around the same time, but Benz patented his first.

So it was that when Benz patented his three-wheeled **MOTORWAGEN**, or motor carriage, in 1886, the car sprang to life.

When the first cars were driven on roads in the 1890s, people had only just got used to the idea of moving images in cinemas and music being played through a gramophone. The early cars were some of the most exciting inventions around, and people clamoured to catch a glimpse of one.

Cars for the Rich

NOT TO BE OUTDONE, DAIMLER SOON STRUCK UP AN AGREEMENT
WITH FRENCH MOTOR COMPANY **PANHARD ET LEVASSOR**.

They were to manufacture cars using Daimler's engine
design. The first models went on sale in 1892. At that
time, the average person earned around £50 per year, so
at £1,000 each, only the very wealthy could afford a car.

The privileged owners of these early cars treated them in
a similar way to their horse-drawn carriages, by having a
servant or chauffeur drive them. It was a difficult job for
the driver, because the brakes were weak, the engine was
unreliable and the road surfaces were rough and uneven.

It wasn't long before cars started
to become more widely popular in
Britain and the USA, especially
when the Prince of Wales – the
future King Edward VII – was seen
in his British-built **DAIMLER** in 1900.

One of the first people to market cars successfully was
Emil Jellinek, who sold **DAIMLER** cars under the brand name of
MERCEDES ... which happened to be the name of his daughter!

1900

Faster, Cheaper, Better

MOST THINGS WE BUY TODAY ARE MASS-PRODUCED IN FACTORIES. BUT IN THE LATE 1900s, MANY PRODUCTS WERE STILL MADE BY HAND — INCLUDING CARS.

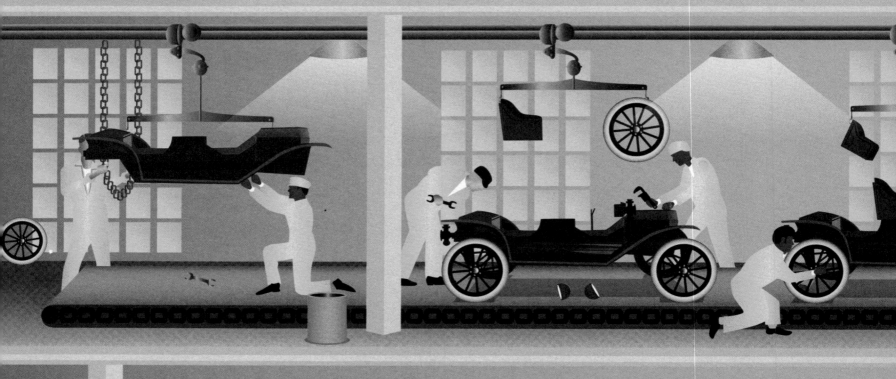

Cars were built one at a time, which made the process time-consuming, complicated and expensive – too expensive for most people. This started to change in 1894, when Karl Benz made several dozen identical **VELO** cars. However, it was American designer Henry Ford who transformed the way cars were made.

When he created his **MODEL T** in 1908, he made it simple to drive and cheap to repair. But at $850 (then about £175), a **MODEL T** was still pricey. So Ford didn't stop there. He realised that an assembly-line technique could speed up production.

In 1913, he introduced moving assembly lines with conveyor belts in his factory in Detroit, USA. The number of cars the factory could build increased dramatically, but even then, Ford continued to find ways to make car production faster. He discovered that black paint dried quicker than any other colour, so he decided to sell only black cars.

By 1914, sales of Ford's trusty **MODEL T** had rocketed to 250,000 vehicles a year, and by 1916 he was able to reduce the price to $360. With such a low price, over fifteen million **MODEL Ts** were sold by 1927. The car was no longer for the wealthy; it was for everyone.

1908

Follow the Leader

BY THE 1920s, CAR COMPANIES AROUND THE WORLD WERE COPYING **FORD'S** MANUFACTURING TECHNIQUES AND CAR PRICES BEGAN TO DROP. THIS COINCIDED WITH THE GROWTH OF THE MIDDLE CLASSES, WHO HAD MONEY TO SPEND ON LUXURIES SUCH AS CARS.

In France, **CITROËN** created its **5CV TYPE C** for women drivers in 1922. It was a small car with an electric starter rather than a manual starting handle. By the mid-1920s, independent-minded women were taking to the road in ever-greater numbers.

1922

The **AUSTIN SEVEN** was released in Britain in 1922. It was a small car, and at just £122, it proved extremely popular. After a few years, the **SEVEN** also became the first widely available second-hand car, which made it even more affordable.

Aircraft-engine builder **BMW** soon gained permission to manufacture the **SEVEN** for German customers, which launched them into the car-making business.

The **SEVEN** was so popular that **NISSAN** copied its design for the basis of their first cars, kick-starting the growth of the Japanese motor industry.

A Day at the Races

THE FIRST KNOWN CAR RACES TOOK PLACE IN 1895.

In the absence of dedicated racetracks, drivers would race on the
roads between cities, such as from Paris to Bordeaux in France.
It was a dangerous pastime – spectators often stepped out in front
of cars, not realising how fast the vehicles travelled!

At first, car races were demonstrations of endurance and reliability. The challenge was
to build a car that could go the furthest distance at the fastest speed with the smallest
number of repairs along the way. In 1900, the 1,000-Mile Trial took drivers from London
to Edinburgh and back. The race took 22 days to complete, and 63 cars set off at the start.
By the end, only 35 were left – the rest had broken down.

In 1907, the world's first car-racing track opened at Brooklands in Surrey, UK. A gutsy driver called Percy Lambert achieved a staggering speed of 166 kph while careering around the track in 1913. But the following year, racing at Brooklands came to a halt with the outbreak of the First World War.

The war ended in 1918, and the 1920s brought with them a series of international races called Grands Prix. Countries competed against one another, with each nation's cars painted a different colour. There were mid-race repair 'pits' at the Grands Prix for drivers to pull in to.

In 1923, another race event became popular: the 24-hour race at Le Mans, France. Driving a car 'round-the-clock' was seen as the ultimate challenge, both for the teams of drivers and the cars, which had to be extremely reliable to stand a chance of finishing. Spectators partied through the night as they cheered the cars along! Le Mans has been held annually ever since, except in 1936 due to French strikes, and from 1940 to 1948 due to the Second World War.

The World Wars

IN THE FIRST PART OF THE TWENTIETH CENTURY, TWO DEVASTATING WORLD WARS ERUPTED. FROM 1914 TO 1918, AND FROM 1939 TO 1945, MOST CAR MANUFACTURERS HAD TO START MAKING MACHINES THAT WOULD HELP WIN WARS.

In the First World War, cars were modified into ambulances and special vehicles were built, such as armoured cars, lorries and aeroplanes. **RENAULT** built 3,600 **FT TANKS**, and their speed and number made a considerable difference to the war effort.

When the Second World War broke out in 1939, manufacturers again used their factories to build thousands of military vehicles. **ROLLS-ROYCE'S** engines powered the **SPITFIRES**, **HURRICANES** and **LANCASTER BOMBERS** that flew in the skies of Europe and Asia.

This focus on military manufacturing made car factories an important enemy target. The **VOLKSWAGEN** factory at Wolfsburg in Germany was almost bombed to ruin, but the British Army rebuilt it to start making one of the most famous cars of all time: the **BEETLE**.

The **JEEP** was invented in 1940 for the US Army. Originally styled 'GP' (short for 'General Purpose'), the light four-wheel-drive design was created in just seven weeks. It became an essential part of military action on land: **JEEPS** were used to lay telephone wires, carry the

Lives of Luxury

DESPITE THE FINANCIAL PRESSURE OF THE GREAT DEPRESSION, THE 1930s SAW CUSTOM-MADE CARS BECOME MUST-HAVE STATUS SYMBOLS FOR HOLLYWOOD STARS AND ROYAL FAMILIES AROUND THE WORLD.

Luxury brands such as **ROLLS-ROYCE** or **BUGATTI** supplied a bare frame with wheels, an engine and a steering capability, but no seats, doors or windscreens. This bare frame, known as a chassis, was then sent to skilled craftsmen who would build the body by hand to the customer's exact requirements. The finished car might be a two-seater sports car or a seven-seater limousine!

Indian maharajahs ordered some of the biggest and most spectacular vehicles. Their sumptuous interiors would include deeply padded seating, thick velvet curtains and elaborate hand-painted décor.

However, custom-made cars were extremely expensive. A single car could cost up to thirty times an average annual salary, so the demand for them slowly died out. Eventually, the separate chassis frame and body were eliminated in most cars and replaced by a single structure called a monocoque.

In the early 1930s, **CITROËN** used the breakthrough idea of the monocoque for its **TRACTION AVANT,** to make it one of the first cars with front-wheel drive. By the 1950s, monocoque design was a standard feature: the all-in-one structure made cars stronger and safer, as well as giving them a smoother ride with less vibration.

1934
Streamlined Design

WHEN AEROPLANES FIRST TOOK TO THE SKIES, AVIATION DESIGNERS STUDIED HOW THE SHAPE OF AN AIRCRAFT CHANGED THE WAY AIR MOVED PAST IT. CAR MANUFACTURERS REALISED THIS INFORMATION COULD BE USEFUL FOR THEM, TOO. IF THEY COULD DESIGN VEHICLES IN A WAY THAT REDUCED WIND RESISTANCE, CALLED STREAMLINING, THEY COULD ACHIEVE GREATER SPEED AND STABILITY.

In 1934, the world's first highly aerodynamic car went on sale: the Czechoslovakian *TATRA T77*. To reduce wind resistance, the bulky engine was moved to the back, the headlights were smoothed into the body and the windscreen was sloped backwards. A few miscalculations meant that the car swayed slightly when it was driven at high speed, so the designers attached a fin to the back of the vehicle. This made it look a bit like a shark, but succeeded in keeping the car steady on the road!

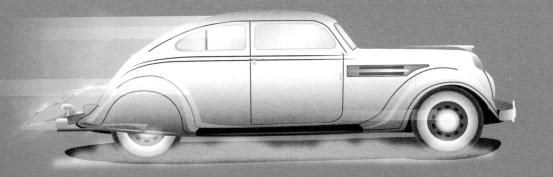

The introduction of the *T77* meant that cars were starting to look different. However, customers didn't approve of rounded, aerodynamic designs. When *CHRYSLER* launched the *AIRFLOW* in 1935, sales were poor, because its look was so different to the cars people were used to.

AERODYNAMIC TESTING

Car manufacturers persisted though, and aerodynamics became an important part of car design. To check how streamlined their cars were, designers built wind tunnels: cylindrical chambers with powerful fans that blew gusts of wind over the vehicles. Today, beams of coloured smoke are used to make the flow of air visible, helping researchers to understand how to make cars sleeker and faster.

How Cars Changed the World

OVER TIME, THE CAR GRADUALLY BECAME SO POPULAR THAT THE WORLD AROUND IT NEEDED TO CHANGE. ROADS — MANY OF WHICH WERE THOUSANDS OF YEARS OLD — WERE UPDATED, SO THEY COULD HANDLE THE INCREASING NUMBER OF CARS. TRAFFIC LIGHTS HELPED TO CONTROL THE FLOW OF TRAFFIC.

As roads became busier, they also became more dangerous. Governments decided that anyone who wanted to drive a car should be thoroughly trained, so in the 1930s, driving tests were made compulsory in Britain.

Driving on country roads wasn't safe or speedy, so in 1924, Italy built the first multi-lane highway, called an *autostrada*. This was quickly followed by *autobahns* in Germany and freeways in the USA, while motorways arrived in Britain much later, in 1958.

Highways meant that drivers could travel across entire countries more easily than before, but they needed something very important to help them do that: petrol. At first, petrol was sold via chemists' shops and simple roadside pumps, but these soon grew into petrol stations that sold oil, tyres and even road maps.

People needed breaks from their long drives, so motels arrived in the USA. These affordable hotels on busy highways were perfect for weary drivers, because they could park right outside their motel rooms. Drive-in movies also became popular pastimes, with rows of cars parked in front of an enormous screen and huge loudspeakers. Waitresses served customers milkshakes, hot dogs and French fries through their car windows!

A Car for Everyone

EACH PERIOD IN RECENT HISTORY HAS SEEN DIFFERENT CAR DESIGNS BECOME POPULAR. FOR EXAMPLE, THE 1950S AND 60S WERE ERAS OF SPORTS CARS. HOWEVER, THROUGHOUT ALL OF THE AUTOMOBILE FASHIONS, THERE HAS BEEN ONE ENDURING TREND: THE SMALL CAR.

In the 1940s, financial pressures after the Second World War meant that small cars were the most affordable. By the 1950s, there was a surge in the growth of the middle classes, particularly in the USA. These families wanted to purchase cars for the first time, but on a limited budget. Tiny cars, such as the *ISETTA*, were popular. This car had an engine from a motorbike, and was so small that it was nicknamed the 'bubble car'. The whole front of the car hinged open as a single door.

Perhaps the most famous economy car of all is the *MINI*. This iconic car, first released in 1959, was cleverly designed. The engine was positioned sideways, so that four people could fit inside a car less than 3 m long. Fun to drive and super-stylish, the *MINI* quickly became a family favourite.

1940

1950

1960

In the 1960s, the wide success of 'kei' cars in Japan led to a huge surge in sales. The kei cars' small engines made them affordable for many. Almost overnight, the average Japanese person could afford to buy a car – and they did. Japan was on track to become one of the world's leading car manufacturers.

Computers in Cars

THE FIRST CAR TO INCORPORATE A COMPUTER WAS THE **VOLKSWAGEN 1600**, RELEASED IN 1967. EVER SINCE THEN, SOME OF THE MOST EXCITING INNOVATIONS IN MOTORING HAVE BEEN BASED AROUND COMPUTER TECHNOLOGY.

AIRBAGS

MERCEDES-BENZ introduced these as standard equipment in 1981. With sensors to detect sudden changes in force, airbags can inflate in a split-second to cushion occupants if their car is involved in a crash. Today, each vehicle has at least two airbags and some cars have as many as 12.

AUTOMATIC PARKING

Many cars have parking sensors, which make it easy for automated systems to squeeze them into the smallest of spaces.

SATELLITE NAVIGATION

Satnav combines satellite tracking and digital information to pinpoint a driver's location on a map and guide them to their destination. In 1990, **MAZDA'S EUNOS COSMO** was the first ever mass-produced car to have a built-in GPS navigation system.

CRUISE CONTROL

Modern cruise control was invented by Ralph Teetor in the late 1940s. His inspiration came after a frustrating car journey, when Teetor noticed that the driver slowed down when he was talking and sped up when he wasn't. He created a device to control a car's speed automatically, which was introduced in 1958.

1997

Effects on the Environment

MOST PEOPLE USE CARS EVERY DAY, WHICH IS A BIG PROBLEM: THEY CAN BE VERY BAD FOR THE ENVIRONMENT.

The petrol or diesel burned inside engines give off waste gases. These include carbon monoxide and unburned hydrocarbons, which can be damaging to the Earth's atmosphere, as well as being dangerous to humans. Pollutants like these are usually invisible, but on hot days, places with heavy traffic often show them in the form of smog.

Improved fuel quality, better engine design and the introduction of exhaust filters mean that a modern car is fifty times more environmentally friendly than one built in the 1970s. But burning fuel is never good for the environment, and our supply of fossil fuels can't last forever – so other ways to power vehicles are now being developed.

In 1997, **TOYOTA** launched the **PRIUS**. It was the first mass-produced hybrid car to have a petrol engine for long journeys and an electric motor for shorter ones. Newer hybrid cars, such as the **TESLA**, can travel up to 650 km before needing to be recharged, and their petrol engines only act as a back-up.

A Need for Speed

JEANTAUD
1898

Gaston de Chasseloup-Laubat, **PARIS, FRANCE**

FORD 999
1904

Henry Ford, **MICHIGAN, USA**

SUNBEAM
1924

Malcolm Campbell, **SOUTH WALES, UK**

CAMPBELL-RAILTON BLUEBIRD
1935

Malcolm Campbell, **UTAH, USA**

BLUEBIRD-PROTEUS CN7
1964

Donald Campbell, **LAKE EYRE, AUSTRALIA**

BLUE FLAME
1970

Gary Gabelich, **UTAH, USA**

THRUST SSC
1997

Andy Green, **NEVADA, USA**

BLOODHOUND SSC
2017

British fighter pilot Andy Green is hoping to be the first driver to break the 1000 mph mark – beating his current world record – in the jet- and rocket-propelled **BLOODHOUND SSC**. The first test runs are currently slated to take place in South Africa in 2017.

THE QUEST TO ACHIEVE SPEED, SPEED AND MORE SPEED HAS BEEN
AN OBSESSION FOR DRIVERS EVER SINCE THE CAR WAS INVENTED.

39 mph

63 kph

91 mph

146 kph

146 mph

235 kph

301 mph

484 kph

403 mph

649 kph

622 mph

1001 kph

763 mph

1228 kph

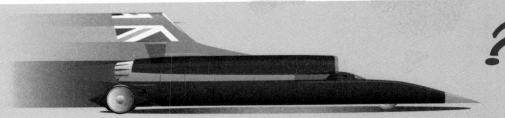

?

A Modern Car

THE AUTOMOBILE HAS COME A VERY LONG WAY SINCE KARL BENZ FILED HIS PATENT IN 1886. EVERY ELEMENT OF A CAR IS NOW METICULOUSLY DESIGNED AND ENGINEERED TO ACHIEVE THE BEST POSSIBLE PERFORMANCE.

BATTERY

The car's electrical equipment is powered by a big battery, which charges when the engine runs.

ENGINE

The power unit is usually fitted at the front of the car, although sports cars often have theirs behind the driver.

FRONT GRILLE

This slatted panel allows air in, so the engine does not overheat.

BRAKING SYSTEM

The driver operates the brakes using a floor pedal. Metal discs with pads on them are pushed outwards to slow the wheels down using friction.

GEARBOX

This controls the speed at which the engine turns. The driver operates it via the gear lever inside the car, choosing the right gear for accelerating uphill or cruising on a motorway. An automatic gearbox selects the right gear for the driver.

DASHBOARD

This is the information interface for the driver, displaying details such as the current speed, fuel level and engine temperature.

DRIVE-SHAFTS

These usually take power from the engine to turn the front wheels; on a rear-wheel drive car, a different shaft takes power to the back wheels. Four-wheel drives have both.

PETROL TANK

The storage chamber for the car's fuel is positioned as far away from the engine as possible for safety reasons.

LIGHTS

Headlights are for night driving. Indicator lights, near the car's corners, show other drivers which way the car will turn. Red lights at the back tell drivers following behind that the car is braking.

EXHAUST PIPE

Waste gases exit the engine via this long metal pipe under the car. It has one chamber called a silencer, to cut noise, and another, called a catalytic converter, to filter pollution.

SUSPENSION

Using springs, links and brackets, this system absorbs bumps in the road, so that drivers and passengers have a smoother ride.

WHEELS AND TYRES

Rubber tyres, filled with air, clamp snugly on to the metal rims of the wheels. Their treads are carefully designed to grip the road surface, even in heavy rain.

Designing a Modern Car

MANUFACTURERS CARRY OUT CUSTOMER RESEARCH TO CHECK THAT A CAR THEY ARE PLANNING IS ONE THAT PEOPLE WILL WANT TO BUY. ONCE THIS INFORMATION HAS BEEN GATHERED, DESIGNERS USE DATA AND THEIR EXPERTISE AND IMAGINATION TO CREATE A NEW MODEL.

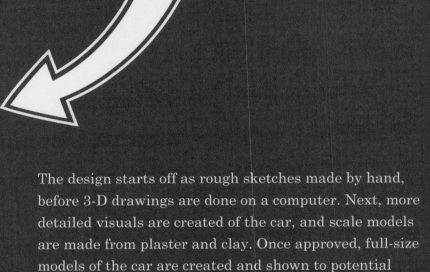

The design starts off as rough sketches made by hand, before 3-D drawings are done on a computer. Next, more detailed visuals are created of the car, and scale models are made from plaster and clay. Once approved, full-size models of the car are created and shown to potential buyers for their feedback.

If the design is right, engineers turn the model into a prototype. Different teams of experts work on the engine, safety systems and the interior features, from the seats to the feel of the buttons. Meanwhile, another team plans how the factory might need to be modified for the car to be built.

Prototypes of the new car will undergo thousands of
kilometres of testing in the hottest and coldest places on earth,
from deserts to the Arctic Circle. Every moving part of the car will
also be tested for durability on specially built machines called test rigs.

Before the car goes on sale, it must pass numerous tests to be certified for use
on the road. It has to be deemed safe for its occupants and other road users, and
its performance and fuel economy must match the claims of the manufacturer.
Only then will the production lines start.

The Making of a Modern Car

CAR FACTORIES ARE ENORMOUS BUILDINGS PACKED WITH AUTOMATED EQUIPMENT THAT CAN TURN A COLLECTION OF CAR PARTS INTO A FINISHED VEHICLE. THE TWO MOST IMPORTANT PARTS OF ANY CAR ARE ITS ENGINE AND ITS BODY STRUCTURE.

The main sections of the engine are split into the lower part, called the block, and the top part, called the head. These are machined from a solid block of aluminium, while the other moving parts are machined, or cast, from strong metals that can withstand the engine's temperatures. Once all the different parts have been made, the engine is assembled.

Meanwhile, steel sheets are fed into enormous pressing machines, which stamp them into the shapes of the body panels, such as the doors and bonnet. The main parts of the car's inner structure – which most people never see – are welded together by robots. Once it has been coated in corrosion protection and painted, the metal skeleton starts to make its way along a slowly moving conveyor belt.

As it passes through specific workstations, the major parts are slowly added: outer panels are fitted, the engine and gearbox are installed, the windows are slotted into place and the seats and dashboard are bolted in. Some of these jobs are done by robots, but many are done by hand, particularly if special equipment has been ordered by a customer.

When the completed car rolls off the production line, it is carefully examined for faults, checked for leaks and given a road test. Only when it's perfect can it be loaded on to transporters for delivery – which sometimes means a long sea journey – to a local car dealer.

The World's Most Popular Cars

SOME CAR MODELS HAVE BEEN SO POPULAR THAT THEIR MANUFACTURERS CONTINUED PRODUCING THE SAME DESIGN FOR DECADES.

① **VOLKSWAGEN BEETLE**
1945–2001
21 MILLION SOLD

Beetles are simple but very robust. The curvy little car, with its engine at the back, was created in 1930s Germany, but eventually had fans around the world.

② **FORD MODEL T**
1908–1927
15 MILLION SOLD

Henry Ford found an easy way to get people to buy more of his cars: he lowered the price until almost anyone could afford one.

(4) **FIAT UNO**
1983–2015
9 MILLION SOLD

No other single small hatchback has been more popular than the spacious Uno. It has been built all over the world.

(3) **VAZ 'LADA'**
1970–2014
14 MILLION SOLD

The Russians needed a super-tough car to withstand freezing cold winters and uneven road surfaces; Italy's Fiat helped them to create it. It didn't need to be beautiful ... just indestructible!

(5) **RENAULT 4**
1961–1994
8 MILLION SOLD

Everything about this eager little car was useful. It had a big rear door so it could be used like a van and it even had seats that could be removed for a picnic!

From Fiction to Reality

SOME OF THE MOST EXCITING CARS EVER DESIGNED ARE FOUND IN BOOKS OR FILMS. THEY FREQUENTLY HAVE FEATURES THAT SEEM IMPOSSIBLE, BUT THAT DOESN'T STOP MANUFACTURERS FROM TRYING TO CREATE REAL-LIFE MODELS THAT DO SIMILAR THINGS.

Chitty Chitty Bang Bang is the star of a book, film and musical, and was first dreamt up by the author Ian Fleming. It is a car that can drive on roads, float on water and even fly in the air. Real-life flying cars, such as the **MOLLER SKYCAR**, have been proven to work, but they haven't gone on sale yet ... probably because anyone using one would need a pilot's licence!

Ian Fleming also thought up countless gadget-packed cars, to be driven by his secret-agent character, James Bond. From the ejector seat in the **ASTON MARTIN DB5** to the **LOTUS ESPRIT'S** ability to turn into a submarine, most of these amazing modifications are considered too dangerous for the general public.

In 1969, movie-goers around the world fell in love with Herbie, the cheeky **VW BEETLE** with a mind of his own. Japanese manufacturers such as **TOYOTA** have experimented with cars that seem to have a personality, and have even used lighting to create a 'face' on the front of cars.

One of the most iconic cars in global cinema is the **DELOREAN DMC-12**
from *Back to the Future*. The **DELOREAN** has amazing flip-up doors and
an engine that is powered by rubbish. Today, some cars can burn
bio-fuels that are made from waste products, such as used cooking oil.
However, there is one feature of the **DELOREAN** that is unlikely
to be replicated: its ability to travel through time!

Cars of the Future

WE ORIGINALLY FELL IN LOVE WITH CARS FOR GIVING US FREEDOM AND SPEED, BUT WE NOW NEED THEM TO PROVIDE COMFORT, RELIABILITY AND SAFETY, AS WELL AS BEING ENVIRONMENTALLY FRIENDLY. HOW WILL CAR PRODUCERS ACHIEVE THIS IN THE FUTURE?

Future cars will hopefully have better safety records, because they will be harder to crash. They will all have telematics services that combine radar, sensors and automatic adjustment of speed and brakes.

Manufacturers have realised that aluminium and other lightweight materials make cars more efficient, so cars will become lighter. Hydrogen cars powered by fuel cells that produce only water vapour could also reduce environmental impact. They could become as common as petrol cars if a network of hydrogen refuelling stations is built.

Technology is gradually reducing the need for human drivers at all; manufacturers such as **TESLA** have already designed self-driving cars. Scientists have also developed car 'strings', with one lead vehicle at the front controlling a convoy of vehicles behind it.

Eventually, experts predict that we won't even own cars, let alone drive them. When we want to go somewhere, we'll order a pod-like car using an app, and it will arrive at our front door to take us wherever we want to go while we work, relax or sleep inside.

A Short History of the Car

SINCE THE CAR BEGAN ITS JOURNEY MANY YEARS AGO, IT HAS EXPERIENCED PLENTY OF SIGNIFICANT MILESTONES.

The first high-speed road for cars opens between Milan and Varese in Italy.

Henry Ford installs the first moving assembly line in his factory in Detroit, USA.

Transistor radios are fitted to US cars for the first time.

The first call is made on a Motorola in-car radio-telephone.

MERCEDES-BENZ releases the first car with a diesel engine.

The first purpose-designed petrol station opens in St Louis, USA.

1905 **1913** **1924** **1936** **1946** **19**

The first car 'packaged' to be small but roomy, the **MINI**, is launched.

The **LAMBORGHINI COUNTACH** is the first extreme concept car to be offered for sale.

AUDI'S turbocharged **QUATTRO** coupé is the first all-weather high-performance car.

TOYOTA launches its **PRIUS** hybrid, the first mass-market eco-car.

The first **TESLA** electric car is launched; it can travel more than 320 km on a single charge.

55

1959

1974

1980

1997

2008

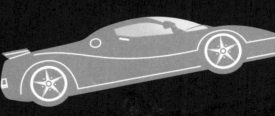

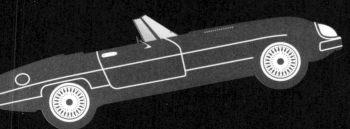

Glossary

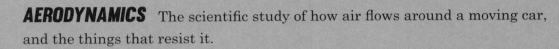

AERODYNAMICS The scientific study of how air flows around a moving car, and the things that resist it.

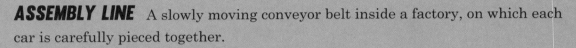

ASSEMBLY LINE A slowly moving conveyor belt inside a factory, on which each car is carefully pieced together.

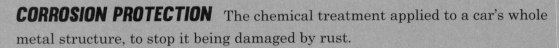

CORROSION PROTECTION The chemical treatment applied to a car's whole metal structure, to stop it being damaged by rust.

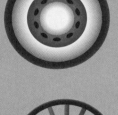

COUPÉ From the French word *couper*, meaning to cut, this is a stylish-looking car with a lowered or sloping roof.

EXHAUST FILTER Also known as a 'catalytic converter', this reduces the amount of harmful pollution petrol or diesel-powered cars release into the atmosphere.

FUEL CELL A fuel-producing system in engines that mixes hydrogen with oxygen to provide power with no harmful pollution.

FUEL ECONOMY A measure of how much petrol or diesel a car needs, given in kilometres-per-litre or miles-per-gallon.

GPS Short for Global Positioning System, this is the satellite-guided computer system that makes satellite navigation, known as satnav, work.

HYBRID CAR A car with a combination of electric and petrol or diesel power, usually designed to suit either short or long journeys.

HYDROCARBON A type of chemical produced after burning fossil fuel inside engines. These chemicals are bad for human health and the environment.

KEI CAR A tiny car designed for Japan's crowded streets, under 3.4 m long and with a small engine.

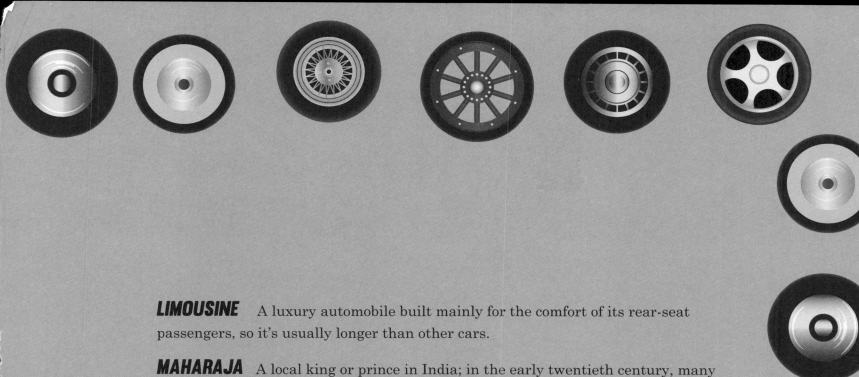

LIMOUSINE A luxury automobile built mainly for the comfort of its rear-seat passengers, so it's usually longer than other cars.

MAHARAJA A local king or prince in India; in the early twentieth century, many maharajas loved expensive cars.

MIDDLE CLASS People who are neither very wealthy nor in poverty, but who enjoy a comfortable lifestyle; car makers try to target their spending power.

MONOCOQUE A car structure which combines the supportive frame and the outer shell in one strong unit.

MOTEL An affordable hotel built for drivers, often where you can park right outside your bedroom door.

PERFORMANCE Figures that prove how quickly a car can accelerate, its maximum possible speed, and how much fuel it consumes.

PISTON A part inside the engine that moves up and down to turn energy into motion, and make a car move.

STREAMLINING Another word for aerodynamics, although a car that just looks 'streamlined' isn't always very aerodynamic!

TELEMATICS SERVICE Communication signals to a car that control it automatically; helping, for example, to keep a safe distance from hazards.

WIND RESISTANCE Airflow that is held back because of a car's body shape – also known as 'drag'.

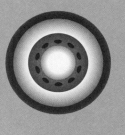

Index